THE MASTERS

101 REASONS TO LOVE
GOLF'S GREATEST TOURNAMENT

❖

RON GREEN, SR.

STEWART, TABORI & CHANG   ❖   NEW YORK

JACK NICKLAUS, SHINGO KATAYAMA, AND JAY HAAS
CROSS THE HOGAN BRIDGE AT THE 12TH GREEN DURING
THE SECOND-ROUND PLAY OF THE 2005 MASTERS.

INTRODUCTION

In April 2007, Augusta National Golf Club awarded me a beautiful plaque carved from a tree that used to stand beside the second tee. It was in appreciation of the 52 times I've covered a Masters tournament.

As much as I appreciated the gesture—the plaque sits in a prominent place near our front door—I felt I should be presenting it to Augusta National for the privilege of walking its fairways watching great players do wonderful things and then getting to tell the readers all about it.

I've covered Super Bowls and Olympic Games and Final Fours and World Series and all sorts of other events, but my true love is the Masters.

Fifty-two Masters mean I've spent a year of my life there, give or take a few days. That's a lot of azaleas. I estimate I've walked 1,000 miles around the course and written a quarter of a million words about what I saw. And I bow to no man when it comes to the number of pimiento cheese sandwiches I've eaten.

Augusta National is Eden with flagsticks, all pines and azaleas and dogwoods and tumbling hills and a creek and little ponds and memories and promises. A place to find beauty and peril entwined, a place to look for ghosts and listen for echoes, a place where anyone who loves golf should be allowed, by some heavenly intervention, to go at least once, to watch Tiger play the 13th, Phil play the 12th.

Many things have changed about the club and the Masters over the years, but at the heart it remains the same—beautiful, challenging, exciting, charming, graceful, cloaked in tradition and history, devoted to the game above all else.

I don't have a plaque to give you who make the Masters happen every year, but please accept this book in appreciation.

—*Ron Green, Sr.*

AN EARLY PHOTOGRAPH OF MAGNOLIA LANE
WITH FIVE GARDENERS.

❶

Magnolia Lane

The tone of the Augusta Masters is set the moment you turn off of Washington Road into Magnolia Lane, the entrance to Augusta National Golf Club. There, 61 magnolia trees, all approximately 150 years old, form a passageway and a canopy leading to beauty, history, tradition, and thrilling competition.

The trees were planted from seed shortly before the outbreak of the Civil War.

Jack Nicklaus, six-time Masters champion, has said of Magnolia Lane, "First time and next time and every time it is absolutely the most sensational drive into a golf course I've ever seen. I get goose bumps every time I drive it."

❷

Welcome Back

Because no patron badges are available to those who don't already have them, it figures that the galleries consist mostly of people who come every year to the Masters, many for decades. Acquaintances are struck up, friendships developed.

There is a feeling of fellowship in an exclusive society, and with each new year, its members come back together, like a family reunion. They will stand in the rain, waiting to get in. They will walk empty fairways when play is suspended. They seem to come as much to be there as to see the golf.

BOBBY JONES DURING PRACTICE AT
AUGUSTA NATIONAL, MARCH 30, 1937.

The Emperor

That is the nickname Robert T. (Bobby) Jones, Jr., earned in a spectacular eight-year surge of golf during which he won 13 of the 21 major championships he entered. Between 1923 and 1930, Jones won five United States Amateur Championships, one British Amateur Championship, four U.S. Open Championships, and three British Open Championships.

In 11 of the last 12 open championships he played—nine U.S. Opens and three British—he finished first or second.

Jones won the Grand Slam of golf in 1930 when he captured the open and amateur championships of both the United States and Great Britain. (Today's Grand Slam consists of four professional titles.)

No player has been more revered than Jones. He was twice accorded a ticker tape parade in New York City. Today, he remains one of the golfers by whom all others are judged. He defined an era. If American golf had a face, it would be his.

Famed golf historian Herbert Warren Wind wrote, "Golf without Bobby Jones would be like France without Paris, leaderless, lightless, lonely."

At the age of 28, weary of the strain and wishing to get on with his life and his law practice, Jones retired from competitive golf, except for an annual appearance in the Masters.

He founded Augusta National Golf Club, where he was named president in 1933 and remains president in perpetuity. He created the Masters, and it was his name on the invitations that first attracted the top players to this new tournament.

4
The Benevolent Dictator

Out there amid the shrubs and tall pines and the echoes of old glories at Augusta National Golf Club, there is a mystery, best one left unsolved. Somewhere out there lie the ashes of Clifford Roberts, who, at Bobby Jones's request, found the site on which this course was built.

It was the stern-faced Roberts, the man great old British golf writer Bernard Darwin described as a "benevolent dictator," who saw to it that the details that would place this course, this club, and the Masters tournament above others, were seen to. He took care of the business and let Jones have the glory. He had enjoyed great success on Wall Street but in time devoted most of his life to the club and the tournament. Byron Nelson said, "This place was his bride."

As chairman, Roberts dismissed more than one member and at least one Masters contestant (Frank Stranahan) on the spot for some violation of protocol.

It was Roberts who directed that sandwich bags and drink cups at the Masters be green so as not to distract TV viewers; who determined that concessions prices be kept low because spectators go to great lengths to attend a tournament and should be offered an affordable meal; who sent out grounds crews to pick up litter all day; who offered amateurs low-cost housing at the club; who kept commercials at a minimum on telecasts of the Masters.

His memoir, *The Story of the Augusta National Golf Club*, was written by Ken Bowden. After he had finished the manuscript, Bowden was summoned back to the club for some additional work on the book. He found that Roberts had brought him back to change six punctuation marks.

Roberts took his own life on Augusta National's par-three course in 1977 at the age of 86 and, in his will, directed that his remains be cremated and his ashes "buried in an unmarked spot on or scattered to the winds over the grounds of Augusta National Golf Club."

In his book *The Making of the Masters*, David Owen wrote of Roberts, "Had he wanted a gravestone, an appropriate epitaph would have been that of Sir Christopher Wren, the architect of St. Paul's Cathedral in London, whose unassuming tomb in the great building's crypt is inscribed '*Si monumentum requites circumspice.*' If you seek his monument, look around you."

Succeeding chairmen of Augusta National were William H. Lane, Hord W. Hardin, Jackson T. Stephens, William (Hootie) Johnson, and William Porter (Billy) Payne.

BOBBY JONES AND CLIFFORD ROBERTS, 1957.

"It seemed that this land had been lying here for years just waiting for someone to lay a golf course upon it."

Bobby Jones

5

A Difficult Birth

The original plan for Augusta National Golf Club called for 1,800 members (about six times the current number), two 18-hole courses (one specifically for ladies), tennis courts, squash courts, an 18-hole pitch-and-putt course, a bridle path, a couple of dozen houses along the fairways for members to purchase, and possibly an on-site hotel.

The plan also called for the manor house to be torn down and a new clubhouse built.

Failure to enroll enough members caused Jones and Roberts to abandon the grand plan and just build a golf course.

After having played Cypress Point, one of the world's greatest courses, Bobby Jones decided he wanted the man who created that California course, Alister MacKenzie, to design Augusta National.

MacKenzie agreed to design the course for $10,000 but lowered his fee to half that when it became apparent that the financial depression gripping the country was going to make it difficult for Jones and Roberts to raise the necessary money.

Work began in February 1932, and in 124 consecutive calendar days, including 18 Sundays and 30 days lost because of wet grounds, the job was completed. Jones offered suggestions along the way.

The club couldn't pay MacKenzie his full fee. Jones and Roberts were having difficulty finding members and were struggling financially. The general public was allowed to play the course to generate money from greens fees.

But as the economy came out from under the depression and began to flourish again, so did Augusta National, and today, membership in the club is among the most coveted and applications are not accepted. Membership is by invitation only.

6

The Clubhouse

Something right out of *Gone With The Wind*. White, three floors, porches, a cupola, shaded by big trees, two chimneys, a sweeping view of the golf course spilling away downhill toward Rae's Creek. Breakfast favorites: country ham and grits with redeye gravy. Dessert of choice: peach cobbler.

Inside, there is much to be experienced: echoes from the past, soft light playing off a trophy; old golf clubs lying in silent rest, having once brought roars from the crowds; remnants of history once touched by Jones and Sarazen and Hagen and Snead and Nelson and Nicklaus and Palmer.

The clubhouse has a certain quiet elegance but it is far from palatial. Its colors are muted, its furniture functional. Were it not for the mantle of greatness that lies over it all, it could be any other fine old country club in America. As one man said, here you feel you can put your feet up and your glass down without a coaster.

Several additions and renovations have been made since it was built in 1854 by the owner of an indigo plantation.

7

A Proper Hanging

Pictures in Augusta National's clubhouse still hang on two hooks because crooked pictures drove Clifford Roberts to distraction. He also favored giving change at the club with nothing but new bills and always carried enough of each denomination to assure that he would not have to accept old bills in change.

8

Granny

At the time Augusta National Golf Club was being founded and promoted to prospective members, Grantland Rice, the country's most famous sportswriter and a glamorous national celebrity, dropped mentions of this new club in some of his columns, which were widely syndicated.

He, Bobby Jones, and Clifford Roberts hoped these mentions might help in recruiting members.

At one point, Rice arranged for a private train to bring members and prospective members to Augusta from New York. Of the 100 who came, though, only one joined the club after a chilly, rainy three days.

Rice, a close friend of Jones, was named honorary chairman of the first Masters.

BOBBY JONES WITH
GRANTLAND RICE
ABOARD THE *S.S.*
EUROPE, 1936.

One of Bobby Jones's best friends was a sportswriter from *The Atlanta Journal* named O. B. (Pop) Keeler, who chronicled Jones's golfing career for his newspaper and wrote press releases for Augusta National.

Theirs seemed a curious relationship, Jones being the shy, dignified, gentlemanly champion and Keeler being the urbane, fun-loving, poetry-spouting writer with a big thirst, but they meshed well.

In the elegant style of the 1920s and 30s, a Detroit newspaper article read, "While Jones composed his epics, Keeler sang them to the world and they seemed all the finer for the manner of singing."

10
The Name

Clifford Roberts, who had helped make Augusta National Golf Club and the Masters a reality, suggested that the tournament be called the Masters, but Jones felt that sounded too immodest and they settled on Augusta National Invitation Tournament.

No matter. Famed sportswriter Grantland Rice referred to it as the Masters Tournament in writing about the first one in 1934. Others did the same.

Jones's title lasted five years before he, realizing that many of the media, players, and public were calling it the Masters anyway, relented.

11
Who Needs Rules?

In one of the early Masters, Bobby Jones's dad, Colonel Robert Jones, was serving as a rules official on the par-three 12th hole. A player hit a shot into a soggy area near Rae's Creek, which fronts the green, and asked for a casual water ruling.

Colonel Jones asked the fellow how he stood in relation to par.

"Eighteen over," replied the man.

"Then what the hell difference does it make?" snapped the colonel. "Tee the thing up on a peg for all I give a hoot."

BOBBY JONES MISSES A
20-FOOT PUTT BY AN INCH IN
THE SECOND-ROUND PLAY OF THE
FIRST MASTERS TOURNAMENT.

HORTON SMITH PREPARES
TO SIGN HIS WINNING
SCORE CARD.

12

Raising the Curtain

The first Masters was played in 1934. It attracted about 10,000 people for the week, many of them from distant states. The big draw was Bobby Jones, coming out of a four-year retirement to play competitively again. He shot 76–74–72–72—294 to tie for 13th place.

Horton Smith shot 284 and won a first prize of $1,500.

13

Miracle at the 15th Hole

After playing the last eight holes four under par, Craig Wood was being congratulated as the 1935 Masters champion and the committee was preparing to issue his winner's check. Gene Sarazen was the only player left on the course who could catch him, and Sarazen was three strokes behind with four holes to play.

But word reached the clubhouse that the game was still on.

Sarazen had holed a 220-yard four-wood shot for a double eagle at the 485-yard par-five 15th hole. He parred the last three holes to tie Wood at 282 and won the 36-hole playoff by five shots.

That four-wood shot remains one of the greatest ever.

Sarazen won $1,500 and was given a $50 bonus for the 36-hole playoff. He complained that he had to give his caddy, Thor (Stovepipe) Nordwall, more than that.

14

The First Cart

In 1963, Horton Smith, who won the inaugural Masters in 1934, was allowed to use a cart because of ill health. He shot 91–86 and missed the cut. Three decades later, a man named Casey Martin would win a court decision that allowed him to ride in a golf cart while playing in PGA Tour events.

ARNOLD PALMER PUTTS ON THE 13TH GREEN
DURING THE FINAL DAY OF PRACTICE FOR
THE 2004 MASTERS.

The Back Nine

What is now the second nine on Augusta National was originally the first. The switch was made because the shady area near what is now the 12th green, which lies at the lowest elevation on the property, was the last part of the course to thaw on frosty mornings. By playing the other side first, golfers could tee off earlier.

It was a fortunate decision. Jones wanted a course that was demanding but offered tantalizing opportunities for scoring, and that's what he got, especially on the back nine. On Sunday afternoon, when the battle is raging, great roars or loud groans can be heard as the patrons cheer birdies and eagles and lament wayward shots. The champion is almost always a player who took risks back there.

Jones said, "We have always felt that the make-or-break character of many of the holes of our second nine has been largely responsible for rewarding our spectators with so many dramatic finishes. It has always been a nine that could be played in the low 30s or the middle 40s."

"If there's a golf course in heaven,
I hope it's like Augusta National.
I just don't want an
early tee time."

Gary Player

Lord Byron Reigns

In the 1937 Masters, a handsome young
Texan named Byron Nelson made up six
strokes on Ralph Guldahl over two holes the
final day and won by two strokes. Guldahl
played the par-three 12th and par-five
13th holes in 5-6. Nelson played
them in 2-3—birdie, eagle.

The Nelson Bridge at No. 13
was dedicated in 1958 to honor
this feat.

Lord Byron vs. Bantam Ben

When they were young boys, Byron Nelson and Ben Hogan worked as caddies at the same club in Texas. They also played against each other for the caddy championship, with Nelson winning in a nine-hole playoff.

They met again in a playoff in the 1942 Masters. After tying for first place at 280 after 72 holes, they played off on Monday. Hogan took a three-shot lead over the first five holes and played one under par from there in, but it wasn't good enough. Nelson played the last 13 holes five under par to win 69–70.

It was Nelson's second Masters championship. He won $1,500. Only the top 12 finishers won money.

18

Sleep Talking?

According to a newspaper story appearing during the Masters in 1942, after Byron Nelson announced he had discovered the secret to playing the difficult Augusta National course (but wouldn't tell his colleagues what it was), Ben Hogan approached Mrs. Nelson at breakfast and said, "I don't want to appear nosy but by any chance did Byron talk in his sleep last night?"

⑲

Augusta National Farm

With World War II raging, the Masters tournament was suspended from 1943 through 1945 and the club was closed. To help with the war effort and to raise money to help sustain the club while no dues were coming in, Clifford Roberts hit upon the idea of raising cattle and turkeys on the property. Some 200 cattle and 1,400 day-old turkeys were purchased and the plan was to increase the cattle population, but the experiment went awry.

The club lost about $5,000 on the beef operation, and that didn't include the damage to the course and its plants caused by what Roberts described as "the voracious appetite of the cattle." A profit was made on the turkeys, but Roberts abandoned the farming experiment, announcing in a letter to members that "we have a better chance as a golf club rather than as live-stock feeders." There was talk of planting corn and peanuts in the parking lot but it didn't happen.

Happy Days Again

When the Masters resumed in 1947, jaunty Jimmy Demaret won his second. He was decked out in canary yellow.

There could have been no more appropriate champion. The country was emerging from the dark days of war and smiling again. People were eager for entertainment. Demaret was the man for the job, a man who loved to sing, a man noted for his joyful manner, and a man especially noted for his rainbow wardrobe.

JIMMY DEMARET AT THE 1950 MASTERS.

> *"As a young man, he was able to stand up to just about the best that life can offer, which is not easy, and later he stood up with equal grace to just about the worst."*
>
> *Herbert Warren Wind*

Bobby's Farewell Appearance

Bobby Jones, afflicted with syringomyelia, a crippling disease of the spinal column, played his final Masters in 1948. The greatness that had earned him the Grand Slam and nine other major titles by the time he was 28 years old had diminished with the years as he limited his competitive golf to the Masters.

He had never contended in his tournament but had returned reasonably good scores until 1948, when he shot a final-round 79 for a 315 total, his worst ever.

The last hole Jones ever played was in a friendly round at Augusta National. So ravaged was his body, he wore a brace on one leg and his arms had lost much of their dexterity. He played the par-four 18th—a hole he could handle with a drive and middle iron in his prime—with three wood shots and a pitch-in. In the clubhouse afterward, with drink in hand, he delighted in telling his cronies how he had parred that hole.

BOBBY JONES TEES OFF ON THE
8TH DURING HIS LAST ROUND
AT AUGUSTA NATIONAL AS
SCHOOIE SCHOO AND
CLIFFORD ROBERTS WATCH.

The Green Jacket

In 1937, members were asked to wear green jackets on the grounds to identify them as guides for those seeking information. In 1949, the club began awarding a jacket to the Masters champion. The first to win one was Sam Snead.

It became customary for the previous year's champion to hold the jacket for the new champion at the presentation ceremony on the lawn.

Members and champions are asked not to wear the jacket away from the club, but some exceptions are made for special appearances by the champion, who is allowed to take his home for one year before returning it to the club, where it is available to him anytime he is on the grounds.

ABOVE: ARNOLD PALMER HELPS 1963 MASTERS
WINNER JACK NICKLAUS DON THE GREEN JACKET.

40 YEARS LATER, TIGER WOODS AND MIKE WEIR CARRY ON THE TRADITION AT THE 2003 MASTERS.

23 Augusta on His Mind

The Masters may be the only golf tournament about which someone wrote a song. Songwriter Dave Loggins was so taken by the ambience at the Masters that he began to form the words of a song while walking the course. The tune is sometimes played on television during the tournament.

24 Colorful Names

Each hole at Augusta National is named for a plant that can be found on it. That project was overseen by Louis Berckman, whose family had owned a nursery on the land where the golf course was built. The names, in order: Tea Olive, Pink Dogwood, Flowering Peach, Flowering Crab Apple, Magnolia, Juniper, Pampas, Yellow Jasmine, Carolina Cherry, Camellia, White Dogwood, Golden Bell, Azalea, Chinese Fir, Firethorn, Redbud, Nandina, Holly.

Some have been called other things by golfers from time to time.

ABOVE: AN EARLY
SCORECARD REVEALS
THAT SOME OF THE
NAMES HAVE
CHANGED.

— 32 —

REDBUD, THE 16TH HOLE.

Ike

When he was president, Dwight Eisenhower became a member of Augusta National. Including trips before he became president, during his presidency, and afterward, Ike visited Augusta National 49 times. There are tributes to him in various places, the most prominent being Mamie's Cottage, named for his wife. It is situated near the 10th tee. The Eisenhowers stayed there during their visits.

Ike also had an office above the golf shop.

Five of the president's paintings hang at Augusta National. And a tree is named for him. There's a big loblolly pine left-center of the 17th fairway, about 210 yards out from the Masters tee. Ike hit so many tee shots into that tree, he proposed at a governors board meeting that it be cut down. Chairman Roberts promptly ruled him out of order and adjourned the meeting. It's now known as Ike's Tree.

During his second visit, the general walked through the woods on the eastern part of the property and upon his return told Clifford Roberts that he had found a perfect place to build a dam if the club ever wished to have a fish pond. Ike's Pond was promptly built where he suggested.

That Sinking Feeling

Shortly after he became president in 1952, Dwight Eisenhower's tee shot on the par-three 12th hole landed short of the green and ended up on a sand bar next to the water.

Clifford Roberts told him, "You can play that ball off the sand bar."

Ike climbed down the bank to his ball and sank past his knees in what turned out to be quicksand. Two Secret Service men jumped down and pulled him out.

Ike went to his cottage to change clothes and came back to finish the round, telling Roberts he would never again take his advice about anything related to golf.

THE 13TH GREEN.

Amen Corner

The most famous three-hole stretch in American golf is the 11th, 12th, and 13th at Augusta National. It's called Amen Corner, a name famed golf historian Herbert Warren Wind gave it. He took it from an old spiritual called "Shouting at Amen Corner."

Amen Corner sits at the foot of a long hill, down where Rae's Creek slices through the course. It's a spectacularly beautiful spot but the wind sings a melancholy song down there.

It's a place where dreams go to die.

It's also a place for heroes. The contender who can get past Amen Corner on Sunday afternoon without a crippling mistake can breathe a sigh of relief and think "Amen."

The 11th hole is a 505-yard par-four that dives downhill to a green protected on the left by a pond. The 12th is a pretty, innocent-looking 155-yard par-three that plays across the creek. One pro described it as "the meanest par-three in the world."

Much of its meanness comes from the wind that swirls down there. The 13th is a 510-yard par-five that crosses the creek twice and doglegs to the left. It's reachable in two with a proper tee shot, but there's a history of broken hearts there.

1958 MASTERS DINNER
(FROM L TO R: CLAUDE
HARMON, GENE SARAZEN,
CLIFF ROBERTS, CARY
MIDDLECOFF, SAM SNEAD,
DOUG FORD, BYRON
NELSON, JIMMY DEMARET,
BOBBY JONES, JACK
BURKE, JR., CRAIG
WOOD, BEN HOGAN,
HORTON SMITH, HERMAN
KEISER, HENRY PICARD).

Champions' Dinner

Every Masters Tuesday since 1952, when Ben Hogan
conceived the idea, the previous year's champion
hosts former champions at a dinner in the club. The
champion gets to choose the menu, which sometimes
makes for interesting dining.

Along with fine wine and some priceless story-
telling, dinner has featured, among other things,
Wiener schnitzel (Bernhard Langer); haggis, neeps,
and tatties (Sandy Lyle); wild boar (Mike Weir); and
cheeseburgers (Tiger Woods).

Pimiento Cheese, Please

A favorite of the thousands who come to the tournament every year is the pimiento cheese sandwich sold
at concession stands.

It has become a tradition for some. They'll tell you
the tournament doesn't start until they've had their first
pimiento cheese sandwich of the year. Famed golf
writer Herbert Warren Wind, writing in *The New Yorker,*
called them "fresh and exotic."

There's nothing special about the sandwich; it's just
pimiento cheese on soft white bread, served in a green
wrapper. Although it is quite tasty.

30

Short Shots

The club built a par-three course in 1958, and two years later introduced a par-three tournament for the contestants, to be played on Wednesday afternoon. It has become hugely popular among the patrons.

The players take a lighthearted approach to the event, sometimes letting a child caddy for them, sometimes even inviting a child to putt for them. Holes-in-one are not unusual. The tournament record is 20, shared by Art Wall and Gay Brewer.

Some say it's bad luck to win the par-three tournament. As of 2007, no par-three winner had gone on to win the Masters in the same year.

31

Skipping Along

It has become traditional during practice for players to intentionally skip their tee shots across the water and onto the green at the par-three 16th hole to entertain the patrons.

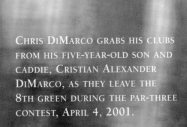

CHRIS DIMARCO GRABS HIS CLUBS FROM HIS FIVE-YEAR-OLD SON AND CADDIE, CRISTIAN ALEXANDER DIMARCO, AS THEY LEAVE THE 8TH GREEN DURING THE PAR-THREE CONTEST, APRIL 4, 2001.

Ornamentals

Azaleas are almost synonymous with the Masters, because they are in such abundance around the course and usually are in bloom during Masters week. There are more than 30 varieties of azaleas on the course. There are also several strains of dogwood and dozens of varieties of ornamental shrubs.

On the golf course side of the clubhouse stands "the big oak." It was planted when the clubhouse was completed in the late 1850s. It is one of the favorite gathering places during the tournament.

Near the big oak is an aspera tree on which a huge wisteria vine clings. It is reported to be one of the first wisteria to be established in this country and is believed to be the largest vine of its kind in the United States.

33

Ballad of Billy Joe

The name, Billy Joe Patton, sounded like something out of a country song. His charming, endearing manner had the feel of the Southern foothills. His golf swing looked homemade. He sold lumber for a living and played golf not for money but for the way it felt.

When Patton came down from Morganton, North Carolina, to Augusta to play in the 1954 Masters, having barely made the field as a Walker Cup alternate, there was little about him to suggest what was to come over those four days.

The lumberman with the blurred backswing tied for the lead in the first round, led after two, fell five shots behind Ben Hogan in the third, then roared back on Sunday. He was playing brilliant golf, including a hole-in-one on the 6th, and after 12 holes, he was three shots ahead of Sam Snead and one ahead of Hogan. On the par-five 13th hole, he found water and wound up with a double bogey. Still playing daring golf, he gambled from a bad lie and a long way out, went for the 15th green in two and found water again, winding up with a bogey.

At day's end, Hogan and Snead were tied for the green jacket and would play-off the next day, with Snead winning. Patton missed the playoff by one stroke.

PATTON BLASTS OUT OF A TRAP ON
THE FIRST HOLE IN THE FINAL
ROUND OF THE 1954 MASTERS.

OPPOSITE: BOBBY JONES PRESENTS
THE AMATEUR TROPHY TO
PATTON, WHILE HOGAN AND
SNEAD LOOK ON.

SAM SNEAD URGES THE BALL ON AFTER PUTTING
ON THE 16TH HOLE IN THE 1954 PLAYOFF.

Sam and Ben

Ben Hogan won the Masters in 1951, Sam Snead in 1952, and Hogan in 1953. They wound up in a playoff for the title in 1954. It was a rare moment in the history of the game, the two greatest players of their time going head to head.

Snead chipped in from off the green on No. 10 and Hogan stubbed a little putt on the 16th, and when they were done, Hogan had shot 71 and Snead had shot 70 and claimed his third Masters title.

BEN HOGAN CHIPS TO THE 2ND GREEN IN THE FOURTH ROUND OF THE 1954 MASTERS.

㉟

Golden Bell

Lloyd Mangrum called it "the meanest little hole in the world." Jack Nicklaus called it "the toughest tournament hole in golf." They were talking about a pretty little par-three hole that measures just 155 yards and goes by the name of Golden Bell. Rae's Creek runs in front of the green and there's sand front and back, but it looks relatively harmless.

What makes it a round killer, though, is the wind. It swirls down there in the valley, and if you misjudge its speed and direction, which often happens, you're in trouble. One player actually misjudged so badly, he hit over the green and up a steep hill, onto an adjoining course, out of bounds.

Arnold Palmer made a 6 there in 1959 when it appeared he might win his second Masters in a row. Billy Casper had an 8 there, Dow Finsterwald an 11.

The tournament record there, though, belongs to Tom Weiskopf. He hit four balls into the creek fronting the green and scored 13.

Tickets Anyone?

As late as the 1960s, players paraded down Broad Street in downtown Augusta in convertibles to promote the Masters. Tickets were available in the early sixties, priced at $7.50 for Saturday or Sunday admission.

Today, no daily tickets are sold except for practice rounds, and the waiting list for season badges is so long applications are no longer accepted. Acceptance of ticket applications first ceased in 1972. A waiting list began that year and names were last added to that list in 2000.

The Price Is Right

Concession prices at the Masters are probably the most reasonable to be found at any significant sports event. When he was chairman, Clifford Roberts said golf fans go through enough to watch a tournament; they should be offered good food at affordable prices.

All That Glitters

The permanent Masters Trophy, which depicts the clubhouse, was made in England and consists of more than 900 separate pieces of silver. The trophy rests on a pedestal. A champion gets his name engraved on the permanent trophy and is awarded a sterling silver replica along with a gold medal and a green jacket.

The runner-up's name is engraved on the permanent Masters Trophy, and he receives a silver medal and a silver salver. Low amateur gets a silver cup and silver medal, and the amateur runner-up gets a silver medal.

There are other awards: day's low round, crystal vase; hole-in-one, large crystal bowl; eagle, pair of crystal goblets; double eagle, large crystal bowl.

39

Don't Ask

Very little information is found about the membership at Augusta National. You do not apply for membership. You are asked to join. There are no women members, but women have played as many as 1,000 rounds at the club in a single year. The number of members and the cost of joining and paying dues are not generally known.

How many people attend the Masters? That information is not available. No one speaks for the club except the chairman.

DOUG FORD BLASTS OUT
OF THE WATER ON THE
15TH IN THE THIRD ROUND
OF THE 1957 MASTERS.

King of the Groundhogs

When Doug Ford won the 1957 Masters, he was known as "King of the Groundhogs," because of his unstylish play, not a beautiful thing except around and on the greens, where he was a master. Ford himself said, "I have to fight the course, the way a gorilla would go at it."

Sam Snead battled Ford to the finish and afterward noted, "His mechanics look something awful but…he does the same thing every time. Ford beats that ol' ball into the ground and don't give a durn whether it gets up into the air or rolls on the ground, just so long as it goes toward the hole."

Lady Luck

In 1963, Ed Furgol's approach shot on the 15th hole hit a woman in the face and bounced back into the water. He made a bogey.

Furgol's response: "I never have had much luck with women."

Good Company

For several years, before pairings and starting times were determined by scores, it was traditional for Byron Nelson to play the last round with the leader or a co-leader. He brought in six winners.

The tradition ended in 1956 when the officials paired third-round leader Ken Venturi with Sam Snead rather than Nelson because Nelson had been Venturi's golf teacher.

Arnie

He was so revered by the Masters' patrons that he once got an ovation when he emerged from the woods after relieving himself.

Arnold Palmer was the most popular player ever in the Masters, outside of Bobby Jones himself. He won it four times, in 1958, 1960, 1962, and 1964, and along the way gave the game a huge surge of energy as the age of television golf was ushered in.

Palmer was a daring, go-for-it player known for his charges. He would snuff his nose, tug at his glove, pull up his pants, and set off down the fairway like a man looking for a fight. His caddy, Iron Man Avery, said, "If Mr. Palmer does that, look out."

In 1958, Palmer eagled the 13th hole to set up his victory. In '60, he birdied the last two holes to win by a shot. In '62, he birdied the 16th and 17th to tie Gary Player and Dow Finsterwald for first place, and in Monday's playoff he played the back nine in 31 to win. In '64, he shot 69–68–69–70 to win by six strokes.

It was in the final round in 1960 that Iron Man asked his unforgettable question. Palmer was struggling and found himself a stroke behind after 15 holes. Upset after a poor pitch on the 15th, Arnie angrily tossed his wedge in the direction of his caddy.

Iron Man glared at him and asked, "Mr. Palmer, are we chokin'?"

Arnie parred the 16th, made a 35-footer for birdie on the 17th and an 8-footer for birdie on the 18th to win by a shot over Ken Venturi.

Little wonder, then, that Augusta is where "Arnie's Army" was born as thousands trailed behind him in every round he played.

Arnie played in 50 Masters before retiring from competition. In 2007, he became an honorary starter, hitting a ball off the first tee to signal the start of play.

Checkmate

In the clubhouse turmoil after he had won his first Masters in 1958, Arnold Palmer asked his wife Winnie to write a check for $1,400 for his caddy Iron Man Avery. Winnie inadvertently made it out for $14,000, which was more than Palmer's prize for winning, which was $11,250.

When Iron Man tried to cash the check at Augusta National, the club tracked the Palmers down at the Town Tavern restaurant to ask if they meant to pay that much.

The mistake was corrected, of course, although probably not to Iron Man's satisfaction.

Honorary Starters

The tradition of having honorary starters, players who are no longer competitive, hit the ceremonial first shots of the Masters began in 1963, with Jock Hutchison and Freddie McLeod. Others who have had that pleasant duty include Byron Nelson, Gene Sarazen, Ken Venturi, Sam Snead, and Arnold Palmer.

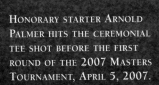

HONORARY STARTER ARNOLD PALMER HITS THE CEREMONIAL TEE SHOT BEFORE THE FIRST ROUND OF THE 2007 MASTERS TOURNAMENT, APRIL 5, 2007.

46

Ben Hogan

When the discussion turns to the greatest players of all time, the name Ben Hogan is invariably on the short list. He won 68 tournaments, including four U.S. Opens, two Masters, two PGA Championships, and the only British Open he ever entered.

But if it can be said of a man who won 2 of them and was in the top 10 in 17 of his 25 Masters, Hogan fell short of expectations at that venue. He won 13 tournaments in 1946 and 10 in 1948, but it wasn't until 1951 that he claimed his first Masters title. Twice before, he had lost the Masters by three-putting the 18th.

He won it again two years later, and this time he showed the course who was boss. Wearing his usual black, gray, and white clothing, locked in concentration and playing in ideal conditions all four days, he shot 70–69–66–69—274 to break the scoring record and win by five shots.

Hogan played on into his fifties, but his putting became so bad, he once said, "I'm not afraid of missing the putt. I'm afraid I can't draw the putter back. When I look at the hole, it's filled with blood."

In 1966, Hogan played his last Masters and made it a memorable one. Then 56 years old, he shot six-under-par 30 on the back nine for a 66 in the Saturday round and wound up finishing in 10th place.

47

Darn That Par

Ben Hogan was not often forthcoming during interviews with the media but he did share a story about a dream that, to some media members, seemed to capture the essence of the great champion. Hogan said he dreamed that he made 17 birdies in a row, then parred the 18th and woke up mad.

The Crow's Nest

Available to amateurs wishing to be housed there during the Masters, the Crow's Nest has living space for up to five people. It's a 30-foot-by-40-foot room with partitions and dividers that create three cubicles with one bed each and one cubicle with two beds. Above the room is the club's cupola.

Typically players stay there for a night or two, for the experience, then move into homes or hotels with their families. Players who have stayed there include Jack Nicklaus, Ben Crenshaw, Curtis Strange, Mark O'Meara, and Tiger Woods.

The Trophy Room

This is the room where members usually have their breakfast and dinner. They sit at their tables eating country ham and redeye gravy or peach cobbler, surrounded by walls housing the implements of some of golf's richest history.

In glass-enclosed cabinets, there is the ball Gene Sarazen knocked into the hole for a double eagle on the 15th in 1935, maybe the most famous shot in golf; a four-wood believed to be the one Sarazen used for the shot; the clubs Bobby Jones used in winning the Grand Slam in 1930, including the original Calamity Jane putter, its leather grip worn, faded, and dry and the clubface, off which rolled some of the most important putts in golf history, dull and faintly dented.

PRESIDENT EISENHOWER
AND HIS CADDIE,
"CEMETERY," AT
AUGUSTA NATIONAL
IN 1953.

Men on the Bag

Until 1983, Masters contestants used caddies provided by Augusta National. After that, they could bring their own.

Some of the local caddies gained a measure of fame with their work. One was William "Iron Man" Avery, who carried for Arnold Palmer in his four victories. Another was Willie "Cemetery" Perteet, President Eisenhower's caddy.

Nicknames have a way of attaching themselves to caddies. Cemetery was known as Dead Man until Ike changed his name. Dead Man resulted from the fact that Perteet had been stabbed by a girlfriend and was left for dead in a hospital morgue before recovering.

Some other nicknames at Augusta National: Skillet, Daybreak, Eleven, Beaver, Marble Eye, Wheezy, Hop, Bull, Stabber, Snipes, Mutt, Fireball, Pookie, Cigarette, Shoo Poon, Eight Ball, Long Distance, Rat, Cadillac, Lamb Chop, Bodiddly.

"Mr. Ike was a pretty good golfer. He wasn't no Nicklaus, no blockbuster."

Willie "Cemetery" Perteet, caddie

The Saddest Masters

A simple bit of arithmetic cost Roberto De Vicenzo, a beloved 45-year-old Argentinian, a chance to win the Masters in 1968.

He shot a final-round 65 and appeared to have tied Bob Goalby for first place, but an error on his scorecard decreed otherwise. Playing partner Tommy Aaron kept De Vicenzo's card during the round and wrote in a four on the 17th hole when in fact De Vicenzo had made a birdie three. When De Vicenzo signed the card, he had to accept the higher number.

Goalby was declared the champion. De Vicenzo said, "What a stupid I am."

Floyd by a Mile

When Raymond Floyd arrived at his locker on Sunday morning in 1976, he was holding the Masters scoring records for the first round (65), 36 holes (131), and 54 holes (201) as well as an eight-stroke lead. He was also holding a Coke in a cup.

He put the Coke on the floor. When he reached into his locker, he dislodged a box of golf balls. The box landed on the Coke and crushed the top of the cup but didn't turn it over.

"I drop a dozen balls on my Coke and don't spill a drop," said Floyd. "See how good I'm going?"

He won by eight, and his 271 total stood as the lowest until Tiger Woods broke it by a stroke in 1997.

ROBERTO DE VICENZO SITS GLUMLY AT
RIGHT, WHILE RAY FLOYD AND BOB GOALBY
SIT AT THE SCORER'S TABLE.

Jack Nicklaus

In 1963, at the age of 23, Jack Nicklaus won his first Masters title and became, at the time, the youngest champion. In 1986, at the age of 46, he won his sixth Masters and became, at the time, the oldest champion.

The last was hailed by many as the greatest Masters, and many would say it was the most heartwarming.

It is memorable because of Nicklaus's age. He was thought by many to be too old to challenge again. Memorable, too, because he played the back nine on Sunday in 30 strokes en route to a 65 that included a run of eagle-birdie-birdie at holes 15, 16, and 17.

In 1965, he set tournament records for 72 holes (271) and margin of victory (nine strokes), including a record-tying 64 in the third round. At the presentation ceremony, Bobby Jones said, "Jack is playing an entirely different game—a game with which I am not familiar."

Nicklaus won a three-way playoff in 1966, becoming the first champion to successfully defend his title. He won his fourth in 1972.

In 1975, in what may have been the best Masters ever from the standpoint of drama and emotion, he sank a 40-foot birdie putt on the 16th hole to secure a one-stroke victory over Weiskopf and Johnny Miller. Tom Weiskopf, pursuing Nicklaus, watched from the 16th tee as Nicklaus ran around the green after holing the long putt, and later said he "had to putt through bear tracks" on that green.

Nicklaus finished his career with 18 career professional major championships.

JACK NICKLAUS HITS AN IRON SHOT DURING PRACTICE FOR THE 1963 MASTER WHILE ARNOLD PALMER AND GARY PLAYER WATCH.

Flying the Flags

Players from around the world are invited to play in the Masters. Flags of the countries represented are flown above the scoreboard to the right of the first fairway. Thirty-five countries have been represented.

Prettying Up

It is estimated that since the Augusta National Golf Club course was built, more than 80,000 plants of over 350 varieties have been added.

Innovations

The leaderboards now used at most tournaments, the type that shows how the player stands with par for the tournament rather than his score on a hole, were first used by the Masters. Roping fairways was also pioneered by the Masters.

Ticketed

Some Masters patrons who have attended a large number of the tournaments decorate their hats with the badges. There can be a dozen or more on one hat. It makes for colorful headgear.

Zeroing In

When Jack Nicklaus revealed at the 1963 Masters that he was using a yardage book, it created quite a stir among the media. It's believed to be the first time a yardage book was used in a major championship.

Nicklaus had learned about using a yardage book a couple of years earlier from friend Deane Beman, who would later be commissioner of the PGA Tour, but had never used it in a pro tournament. Now yardage books are everywhere.

Stonewall

Before the 1967 Masters, when Jack Nicklaus was going for an unprecedented third straight championship, Barbara Nicklaus said, "I think Jack's a little more excited this year than he has been in past years but he controls it well. He has such a wonderful temperament for his profession.

"He is quite emotional, even though he may not show it. He can be at a very high pitch for a round of golf.

"At home, though, he and our oldest son, Jackie, will sit down to watch TV and the house could burn down and they wouldn't know it. I call Jack 'Stonewall,' because he never hears what I'm saying when he's concentrating on television. It's like I'm talking to a stone wall."

Jack's excitement didn't translate into good golf. In a stunning turn of events, he shot 79 on Friday and missed the cut.

JACK NICKLAUS TALKS TO
REPORTERS ON SUNDAY
NIGHT AFTER WINNING
THE 1963 MASTERS.

New Sticks

Billy Casper had played with the same set of woods for 13 years and the same set of irons for 10 years when he got new clubs in 1970. He used the new ones to win the Masters that year.

Chi Chi's Army

In 1964, Arnold Palmer was at the peak of his popularity as he chased, and got, his fourth Masters title. Thousands followed him around, many carrying signs saying they were members of Arnie's Army.

Palmer played one round with Juan (Chi Chi) Rodriguez. Chi Chi would become one of golf's most colorful showmen and beloved figures, but at the time, he was not widely known. There were, nevertheless, some people in their gallery holding signs reading "Chi Chi's Bandidos." Arnie's Army lasted through the years but Chi's Chi's Bandidos didn't.

"Ask any pro what tournament he'd rather win and he'll say the Masters, I'm pretty sure of that."

Sam Snead

The Slammer

One of the most remarkable men ever to play golf was Sam Snead, known as Slammin' Sam. He won his first PGA Tour tournament in 1936 and his last in 1965 at the age of 52.

He is credited with winning 82 Tour events, a record. Seven of those were major championships, three of those majors being Masters titles in 1949, 1951, and 1954. In 1954, he beat Ben Hogan in a playoff, 70–71. For his 1949 victory, he was the first champion to wear the green jacket.

Snead played in 44 Masters, his last in 1983. He had 15 top ten finishes, including a tie for third in 1963 after leading in the final round at the age of 50.

He also starred in the par-three tournament, winning it twice, the second time at the age of 61.

PHOTOGRAPHERS SNAP PICTURES OF SAM SNEAD
DONNING THE GREEN JACKET IN 1949.

63

Amateurs

The Masters has always made way for amateurs, thanks to the influence of the ultimate amateur, Bobby Jones, but no amateur has ever won it.

Charlie Coe, an Oklahoma oil man, tied Arnold Palmer for second behind Gary Player in 1961. Ken Venturi, a San Francisco auto salesman who later won the U.S. Open, finished second to Jackie Burke in 1956.

And Billy Joe Patton, the North Carolina lumberman, missed by one shot of getting into a playoff with Ben Hogan and Sam Snead in 1954.

In the Masters' first 36-hole cut, which came in 1957, five amateurs survived but Hogan didn't.

64

False Alarm

In 1970, a rumor tore through the press room: "Arnold Palmer's had a heart attack on the 13th hole."

A communications man put through a call to central control, reported the rumor, and asked for a check. The reply came back, "Palmer in the 14th fairway, three over par for the tournament. And standing up."

Arnie did have a fractured confidence and a swollen score.

CHARLIE COE

TOM WEISKOPF DROPS HIS
PUTTER AS HIS BALL STOPS SHORT
OF A BIRDIE ON THE 18TH GREEN
DURING THE 1974 MASTERS.

The Avis of Augusta

Tom Weiskopf was one of the most athletically gifted golfers we've seen, but when it came to winning, all too often he came up just short. He may be remembered more for taking a 13 on the par-three 12th hole at Augusta National than for his challenges for the championship.

Four times in seven years (1969, 1972, 1974, 1975), Weiskopf finished second in the Masters. His followers ached for him as he got to the door but never got in.

After Jack Nicklaus won in 1975 in a dramatic battle to the wire with Weiskopf and Johnny Miller, Weiskopf vowed, "Someday, I'm going to win here." He never did.

WEISKOPF MISSES A SHORT BIRDIE PUTT ON 18 ON THE SATURDAY OF THE 1969 MASTERS.

66

The Best Ever

One would be hard-pressed to find a more exciting Masters than the 1975 tournament, because of the three primary contenders, the quality of the golf that was played, and the drama in the closing holes.

Tom Weiskopf had won the week before and said he felt confident from start to finish that he would win the Masters, and he swapped the lead back and forth with Jack Nicklaus around the final 18. Johnny Miller was 11 strokes behind after 36 holes but birdied 15 of the last 36, including six in a row on the front nine on Saturday, en route to a 65, and almost made it reach all the way when he shot 66 on Sunday.

Nicklaus holed a long putt on the par-three 16th and, with Miller and Weiskopf waiting on the tee behind him, ran around the green in celebration, making "bear tracks," as Weiskopf described it.

When it was done, Nicklaus had won but not before Miller and Weiskopf on the last green missed putts that could have tied him.

It was the best.

JACK NICKLAUS AND HIS CADDIE CELEBRATE A
BIRDIE PUTT ON THE 16TH, APRIL 13, 1975.

NICKLAUS SINKS A BIRDIE PUTT ON THE 17TH TO TAKE THE LEAD ON SUNDAY, APRIL 13, 1986.

NICKLAUS SINKS A BIRDIE PUTT ON THE 17TH TO TAKE THE LEAD ON SUNDAY, APRIL 13, 1986.

67

Most Memorable

The Masters is always a compelling story, no matter who wins, but the one that chilled our spines most, that brought happy tears to our eyes, that put a golden crown on the greatest golfing career in history was Jack Nicklaus's victory in 1986.

He had won five Masters, but he was 46 years old and hadn't won a major since 1980, and we thought he was past the time when he could win it again. But on Sunday, with his son Jackie caddying for him, he played the last ten holes seven under par, shooting 30 on the back nine and 65 for the day to win it.

Later, he said in all his years, in all his championships, he had never heard cheers like he heard that day. They are still echoing.

68

Fuzzy

Until 1979, no first-time player had ever won the Masters since Horton Smith won the first one. Veterans would tell you it takes time to learn the course, where to position your tee shot, where not to hit your approaches, how the greens break.

But a cigarette-smoking, wisecracking rookie with a syrupy swing, a Kentuckian named Fuzzy Zoeller, not only won in his first attempt, he did it by beating Ed Sneed and Tom Watson in a playoff.

69

Fairway Follies

Sometimes our heroes can look unheroic. Jack Nicklaus shanked his tee shot on the par-three 12th hole, leaving it short of Rae's Creek. He said it bothered him for a year. The great man also made an 8 on the par-five 8th hole with a lost ball (trees left) and a missed 18-inch putt. He still beat Frank Walsh by four shots on that hole. Arnold Palmer popped up his tee shot on the fourth hole and didn't get halfway to the green.

Tom Weiskopf made 13 on the par-three 12th. That tied Tommy Nakajima's 13 on the 13th hole for highest score on any hole. Jumbo Ozaki, Ben Crenshaw, and Ignacio Garrido each had 11 on the 15th hole, and Herman Barron had 11 on the 16th.

Elusive Glory

Many a man has blown a chance at winning the Masters. It is never pleasant to see. We cheer the champion but hurt for the man who got to glory's door and stumbled.

With rain tapping on his shoulders and Sunday night closing in, Scott Hoch, a face appearing suddenly out of golf's crowd, stood two feet from lasting glory in 1989.

Nick Faldo had already made bogey on the first hole of their playoff. All Hoch had to do to win the Masters was tap in a two-footer. After studying the putt at great length (Ben Crenshaw, watching on TV in the clubhouse, blurted, "Geez! Hit it!") Hoch missed.

Ladies' First

When Elizabeth Archer slung her dad George's clubs over her shoulder in 1983, it marked the first time a woman had caddied in the Masters.

TIGER WOODS CHIPS OUT OF THE SAND ON THE 8TH FAIRWAY DURING THE FINAL ROUND OF THE 2004 MASTERS.

Elder Statesman

No African-American player had ever qualified to play in the Masters until 1975, when Lee Elder made it. He attracted considerable attention from the media early in the week, but Jack Nicklaus, Johnny Miller, and Tom Weiskopf stole the show with the best shoot-out ever in the tournament.

Elder played in six Masters. His best finish was 17th.

Public Relations

With the Masters, it's often a family affair. Ten father-son relations have played in the tournament as have 25 sets of brothers.

There has also been one grandfather-grandson combination: Tommy Armour and Tommy Armour III.

Spanish Conquest

His brother, Manuel, said of Seve Ballesteros's early years playing the game, "He had a love of golf you could almost touch. Without a golf club in his hands, he was a man with no legs. It was a part of him. Without it, he didn't exist."

Seve was the most exciting player since Arnold Palmer and before Tiger Woods. He won two Masters, the first in 1980 at the age of 23. Jack Nicklaus said at the time that Ballesteros had the best chance of anyone of breaking his record of major championships, which then stood at 17.

The Spaniard won again in 1983.

Ballesteros played in 28 Masters and had five top-three finishes. In 1987, he three-putted the first playoff hole to fall out of a battle with Greg Norman and Larry Mize. Mize pitched in on the 11th hole to win.

Seve Ballesteros, asked how he four-putted the 16th hole: "I mees, I mees, I mees again."

Two for Tom

In the early years of his professional career, Tom Watson faltered down the stretch enough to raise speculation that his heart was a poor companion for his exquisite game.

It was, then, especially pleasing to Watson when, after winning his second Masters in 1981, Jack Nicklaus said, "The strongest part of Tom's game is mental toughness." Nicklaus had seen that toughness firsthand in the British Open at Turnberry when the two were paired through the last two rounds and Watson beat Nicklaus over that stretch 65–65 to 65–66. He had also finished runner-up to Watson in the 1977 Masters and again in 1981.

Merry Mex

Lee Trevino, the Merry Mex, won two U.S. Opens, two British Opens, and two PGA Championships but he couldn't solve the Masters. He blamed it on his trademark shot, the low fade, which doesn't suit Augusta National's hills, but Trevino seemed ill at ease at the club. He had some sort of problem with tournament officials and began changing shoes in the parking lot rather than enter the clubhouse. He even quit playing the Masters, but was talked into coming back by Jack Nicklaus.

He did shoot 67 in the opening round in 1989, but followed with a 74 and then blew to 83 on Saturday.

TREVINO REACTS AFTER MISSING A BIRDIE PUTT ON EIGHT, 1975.

TOURNAMENT RECORD

1934	HORTON SMITH	284
1935	GENE SARAZEN AFTER TIE WITH CRAIG WOOD	282
1936	HORTON SMITH	285
1937	BYRON NELSON	283
1938	HENRY PICARD	285
1939	RALPH GULDAHL	279
1940	JIMMY DEMARET	280
1941	CRAIG WOOD	280
1942	BYRON NELSON AFTER TIE WITH BEN HOGAN	280
1946	HERMAN KEISER	282
1947	JIMMY DEMARET	281
1948	CLAUDE HARMON	279
1949	SAM SNEAD	282
1950	JIMMY DEMARET	283
1951	BEN HOGAN	280
1952	SAM SNEAD	286

Bridges, Plaques, and Fountains

The Sarazen Bridge, dedicated in 1955 to honor Gene Sarazen's double eagle in 1935, runs alongside the pond fronting the 15th green. On April 2, 1958, the Hogan Bridge, commemorating Ben Hogan's then-record 72-hole score of 274 shot in 1953, was dedicated at the 12th hole. That same day, the Nelson Bridge at the 13th tee was dedicated to commemorate Byron Nelson's birdie and eagle on the 12th and 13th holes to make up six strokes on Ralph Guldahl and win the 1937 Masters.

In 1995, the Arnold Palmer Plaque, honoring his play and his contributions to the Masters, was affixed to a drinking fountain behind No. 15 tee. Three years later, the Jack Nicklaus Plaque, commemorating his six Masters championships, was affixed to a drinking fountain between holes 16 and 17.

The Record Fountain, left, of No. 17 green displays a progression of course records and the names and scores of Masters champions. The Par 3 Fountain near the No. 1 tee on the par-three course lists the winners of the par-three contest.

Seeing Green

Just about everything at Augusta National is green. Service buildings, garbage bags, sandwich bags, drink cups—name it, it's probably green. And greenest of all is the golf course.

LLOYD MANGRUM, BOBBY JONES, BEN HOGAN, AND CLIFFORD ROBERTS AT AUGUSTA NATIONAL GOLF COURSE TOURNAMENT RECORD FOUNTAIN IN 1959.

The Place to Be

Jack Nicklaus said the 16th hole is the most exciting place in golf on Sunday afternoon.

It's a pretty par-three that plays over water to a sloping green. It's situated in an amphitheater of azaleas and pines close behind the 15th green, and when the action is hot at that juncture, the roars can shake the trees.

Many a Masters outcome has swung on what happened at the 16th. It's where Nicklaus made "bear tracks" in 1965 running around the green after holing a long birdie putt that would prove pivotal. It's where he almost made a hole in one in 1986, unsettling Seve Ballesteros so badly the Spaniard hit an iron shot into the water at the 15th. It's where Tiger Woods made that tantalizing pitch in that went up the hill, then rolled slowly, agonizingly back toward the cup, hung on the lip, then toppled in.

It's where Bert Yancey had a remarkable run of five straight 2s over the span of two tournaments.

It's where dreams can come true, or drown.

The Champions' Locker Room

This room overlooking Magnolia Lane is reserved for former Masters winners. The lockers are of dark wood. For space-saving purposes, many of them are shared. Tiger Woods shares his with Jackie Burke, Mark O'Meara with the late Gene Sarazen, Raymond Floyd with the late Ben Hogan, Bob Goalby with the late Byron Nelson. During tournament week, the champions' green jackets are waiting in their lockers.

Merchandise

So popular is the merchandise building at the Masters, there is a routing system outside to accommodate the lines of patrons waiting to get in. Many make it their first stop, and some take their purchases back to their cars before starting out on the course, although there is a booth where they can leave their packages and pick them up later.

It doesn't seem right to go to the Masters and not bring home something with the logo on it, and maybe a golf shirt for a favorite uncle.

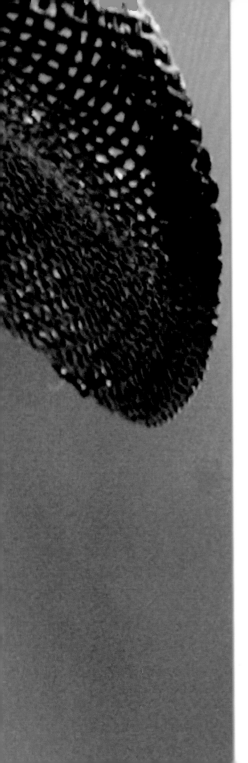

The Shark

His soul is a montage of scars from championships lost. Some he threw away, some were robbed from him. It is a burden no man should have to suffer playing a game.

Greg Norman had it all. He was golf's most glamorous figure, wonderfully talented, devilishly handsome, extremely rich, and a winner of tournaments around the world, including two British Opens. But Larry Mize chipped in to beat him in a playoff at the Masters. Bob Tway holed from a bunker to beat him in the PGA Championship. All in all, Norman was runner-up eight times in majors, losing three playoffs.

It was, nevertheless, a shock when he blew a six-stroke lead in the final round of the 1996 Masters, shooting a 78 and paving the way for playing partner Nick Faldo to win.

When it was done, Faldo and Norman had tears in their eyes and Faldo said, "I just want to give you a hug." And he did.

It Must Be Magic

Anyone who had ever watched play on the 12th hole knew that any shot that landed on the steep bank fronting the green would roll back into Rae's Creek. Never failed.

Well, yes it did, once. Fred Couples came there in the final round in 1992 leading a closely packed field. His tee shot landed just short of the green, bounced back toward the water, and stopped two feet short of the water. Couples said it was the best break he'd ever gotten in golf.

He pitched it up, made par, and went on to win the tournament.

A Storybook Ending

On the Sunday before the 1995 Masters, Harvey Penick, who had taught some of golf's best players and authored the wildly popular *Little Red Book*, died in Texas.

Ben Crenshaw served as one of the pallbearers on the Wednesday before the Masters was to begin on Thursday.

Crenshaw, who had wanted to win for his old friend, played his way to victory, and when the final putt dropped, he immediately bent over, put his hands to his face, and sobbed.

It was one of the most touching moments ever in the Masters, made doubly so by the fondness golf fans felt for Crenshaw, who was often and aptly referred to as Gentle Ben.

GARY PLAYER REACTS WITH A CHEER AS HE SINKS
A BIRDIE PUTT ON THE 6TH GREEN IN THE THIRD
ROUND AT AUGUSTA ON APRIL 8, 1961.

Gary Player

Gary Player has always been generous with superlatives. The greatest course of its kind, he might say. Or the greatest shot I've ever seen. Or the hardest hole in the world. It's just part of his sparkling personality.

He, too, was a superlative. The five-foot-seven, 150-pound South African was the first foreign player to win the Masters. He won it in 1961 when Arnold Palmer, needing only a par on the final hole to win or a bogey to tie, made double bogey from the fairway. Player won it again in 1974, and then in 1978, at age 42 and after having gone four years without a victory in the United States, he closed with a 64 to win his third Masters.

Player also had two memorable second places. He lost to Palmer in a playoff in 1962, and he and Palmer tied for second in 1965 when Jack Nicklaus blitzed the field with a 271 total.

Player, the most widely traveled sports figure in history, won three British Opens, two PGA Championships, and one U.S. Open to go with his three Masters.

GARY PLAYER REACTS AFTER MAKING A LONG PUTT ON THE 2ND HOLE DURING PRACTICE AT THE MASTERS IN 2005.

 86

Rae's Creek

Many a hope has drowned in this pretty little stream that flows in back of the No. 11 green, in front of the No. 12 green, and in front of the No. 13 tee and green.

It was named after John Rae, who died in 1789. It was Rae's house that was the farthest fortress up the Savannah River from Fort Augusta. The house kept residents safe during Indian attacks when the fort was out of reach.

PHIL MICKELSON CHIPS TO THE 11TH GREEN DURING A PRACTICE, 2007.

ABOVE: BRADLEY DREDGE FINDS WATER AT THE 13TH HOLE, 2007.

LEFT: NICK FALDO OF
ENGLAND CELEBRATES HIS
MASTERS WIN OVER RAY
FLOYD ON THE SECOND
HOLE OF SUDDEN DEATH,
APRIL 8, 1990.

87

Faldo and Foldo

Nick Faldo won the Masters three times. He played championship golf each time, but he was also the beneficiary of some notorious stumbles by his rivals.

In 1989, Scott Hoch missed a putt of about two feet on the first playoff hole and lost to Faldo on the next hole. In 1990, the ordinarily steely Raymond Floyd hooked his second shot into the water on the second playoff hole and Faldo won. In 1996, Greg Norman blew a six-shot lead in the final round, shooting 78 to lose to Faldo by five strokes.

What should not be forgotten is that Faldo shot 65 to tie Hoch, then holed a 25-foot putt on the second extra hole to beat him, and while Norman had his flameout, Faldo was shooting 67.

88
Comeback

Dan Pohl shot a pair of 75s in the first two rounds of the 1982 Masters, a performance that many years would have missed the cut, but he wound up in a playoff on Sunday, where he lost to Craig Stadler.

A spectacular surge on Saturday was the thing that propelled him back into the fray. He eagled the par-five 13th and the par-four 14th and birdied the par-five 15th and par-three 16th, en route to a 67.

89
Reserved Seats

It has become a regular practice of Masters patrons to stake out their territory early in the day with canvas seats. They go out and place their seats, walk with the golfers and then settle down into their reserved spot to let the action come to them.

Favorite places are near the 11th green and 12th tee, the 16th hole, and the 18th hole. It's now not uncommon for rows of chairs to run five or six deep.

(There are also bleachers located at many places around the course.)

Welcome Home

After he had birdied three of the last four holes to win the Masters in 1998 and had enjoyed the traditional dinner at the club with the chairman, Mark O'Meara drove back to the house he was renting for the week and found Tiger Woods sitting on the front steps.

Woods, who was O'Meara's neighbor in Orlando, said he just wanted

91

Home Course, Sort Of

The 1967 champion, Gay Brewer, had parked cars at the Masters when he was stationed at Fort Gordon. The 1987 champion, Larry Mize, had helped run the big scoreboard near the 18th green. And Jim Thorpe had caddied at Augusta National.

92

Wanna Fight About It?

Before he became lightweight boxing champion of the world, Beau Jack shined shoes at Augusta National.

93

The Lesson

Shortly before they would hit the ceremonial shots that would herald the start of the 1998 Masters, Gene Sarazen, then 96 years old, Byron Nelson, 86, and Sam Snead, 85, hit a few warmup shots on the practice range.

Sarazen complained about his swing and Snead gave him a short lesson, an 85-year-old legend instructing a 96-year-old legend.

"Try to get your left shoulder under your chin," Snead told him.

Sarazen listened, took three swings, and said, "Okay, that's enough."

Sarazen hit one about 125 yards off the first tee. Nelson hit about 175 yards and well right, reportedly conking a galleryite. Snead's shot went about 220.

STANDING OUTSIDE JONE'S COTTAGE, BOBBY JONES AND PRESIDENT EISENHOWER POSE BESIDE THE PORTRAIT THAT IKE PAINTED OF JONES IN 1954.

Jones's Cottage

The cottage in which Bobby Jones stayed when he was at Augusta National sits just off the 10th fairway. It is a relatively small white house. Its walls are decorated with golfing cartoons, old Scottish prints, a map of the Old Course in St. Andrews, Scotland, where Jones won the British Amateur in 1930, part of his Grand Slam.

The cottage enhances the feeling of Jones's spirit that lies over the Masters.

LARRY MIZE CELEBRATES HIS
1987 MASTERS VICTORY.

Lightning in a Bottle

Something wonderful always happens on Sunday afternoon at the Masters. Roars from the gallery rise into the sky from holes around the back nine. For pure shock, though, probably nothing quite equals the lightning bolt finish Larry Mize brought in 1987.

Some late collapses had earned Mize a reputation as a man who couldn't close the deal, so when he went down the 10th hole, the first hole of a playoff with the world's two most feared golfers of the day, Seve Ballesteros and Greg Norman, his chances looked slim.

But Ballesteros three-putted the 10th hole to fall out. On the 11th, with Norman's second shot resting on the edge of the green, Mize faced a pitch shot of some 40 yards toward a pin standing on the far side of the green, near water. He holed it and began racing around wildly, putter raised, eyes wide. Norman missed his putt and it was over.

A Ticket Home

To the left of the second fairway is a picturesque spot where a little creek ambles through pines and azaleas. It would be okay for a picnic but not for a golf shot.

Over the years, players have referred to it as the Delta Counter. Knock it in there and you might as well ask when's the next flight out of Augusta.

Finding Gold

A small spring in the trees between the 13th and 14th fairways is said to yield trace amounts of gold dust after a heavy rain.

98

Tiger Cub

Tiger Woods first played the Masters in 1995 at the age of 19, when he was still a student at Stanford. He shot 72–72–77–72 and tied with Seve Ballesteros for 45th place.

His score seemed almost inconsequential. Tom Watson watched him and deemed him "potentially the most important player to enter the game in 50 years."

Jim Dent, an African-American playing the Champions Tour, said, "And charisma. He could be like the Jackie Robinsons, and the Willie Mayses and the Michael Jordans in their prime. Believe me, he will be an asset to golf. Tiger doesn't mess around."

Jack Nicklaus said Tiger was capable of winning more Masters than the ten he and Arnold Palmer had accumulated between them.

Visionaries, all.

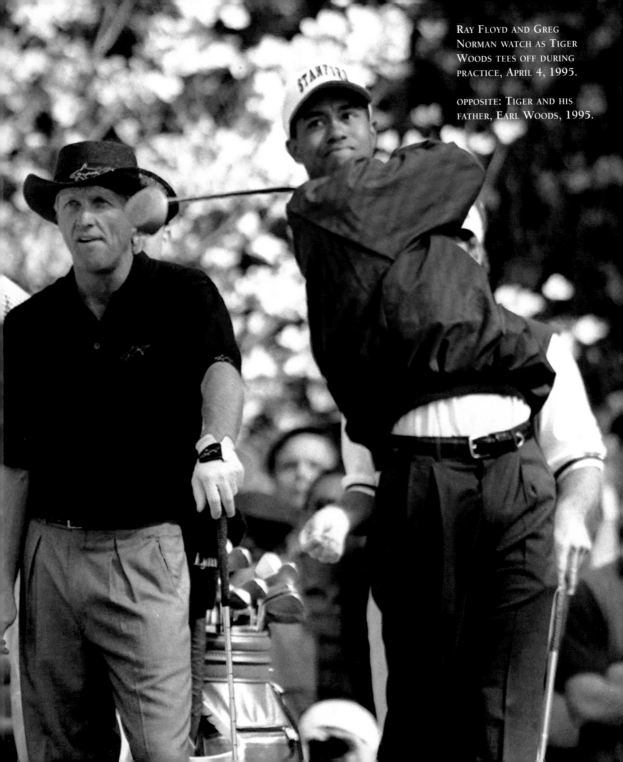

The Man Who Changed Golf

In 1997, with no Nicklaus or Palmer or Trevino or Watson to dominate with their enormous talents, tournament golf in the United States had become a ho-hum affair. No exciting new players had emerged.

Then along came Tiger Woods, with his enormous distance and his wealth of talent and his fine looks and his multiethnic background, and we could not get enough of him.

Augusta National received 500 more requests for media credentials than usual for the 1997 Masters because the young man who had already soared to fame in amateur golf seemed poised to win a historical victory. And he did. He won the Masters and set 20 Masters records and tied 6 others doing it.

It was the most significant victory by anyone in golf since Arnold Palmer won his first Masters in 1958 and triggered an explosion of popularity for the game among the masses.

That week in 1997, Woods shot 70-66-65-69, a stroke better than anybody had ever done it, and he won by 12 strokes.

By 2007, he had won four Masters and there was little doubt that more were to come.

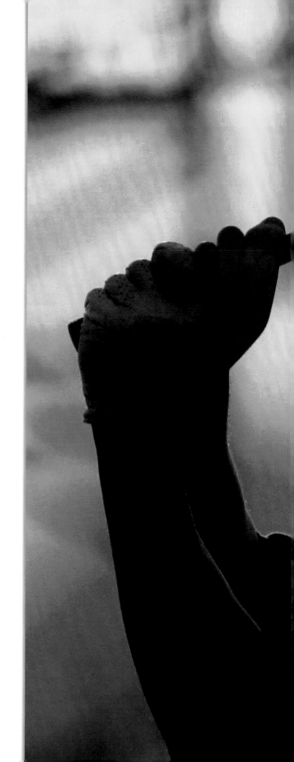

Lefty

When he arrived in Augusta in 2004, Phil Mickelson, a hugely popular and richly gifted left-hander, was known as the best player never to have won a major championship. He had played in 42 of them without a win.

He had finished third in the previous three Masters but had never quite gotten over the hump.

Lefty took care of that with scores of 70–72–71–67, holing an 18-foot birdie putt on the final hole to edge out Ernie Els and punctuating it with a leap for joy. Only three other players had birdied the last hole to win the Masters.

Two years later, Mickelson won again, closing with a 69 for a 281 total that was two shots clear of second-place Tim Clark. This time, he had a chance to enjoy it more. He had a three-stroke lead when he came to the 18th hole.

"The stress-free walk up 18 was incredible," he said. "I'd wanted that. I had actually wanted like a four- or five-shot lead. It was a great feeling walking up there knowing I had the tournament in hand."

Mickelson has long enjoyed the adulation of golfing galleries. His followers rival Tiger Woods's because he plays a daring game and smiles a lot. Their rivalry seems destined to stay hot for many years.

PHIL MICKELSON CELEBRATES AFTER WINNING
THE MASTERS GOLF TOURNAMENT WITH A NINE
UNDER PAR, APRIL 11, 2004.

ARNOLD PALMER WALKS UP THE
16TH FAIRWAY ON HIS FINAL
MASTERS ROUND IN 2004.

101

Encore, Forever

When the last putt has dropped and
the sun is setting on Masters Sunday,
any sense of loss is tempered by the
knowledge that they're going to do it
again next year, same time, same
place, same azaleas, same pines,
same hills and valleys, same aura.
It's a nice thought.

Acknowledgments

Among my collection of golf books are several about the Augusta Masters. I have used some of them in compiling this book, checking facts, looking for ideas I may have overlooked, and in some cases, borrowing quotations.

They are the *Masters Media Guide*, compiled under the supervision of Glenn Greenspan, Augusta National Golf Club's director of communications; *Men on the Bag*, by Ward Clayton; *The Making of the Masters*, by David Owen; *The Story of Augusta National Golf Club*, by Clifford Roberts; *Augusta, Home of the Masters Tournament*, by Steve Eubanks; and my own compilation of stories from the Masters, *Shouting at Amen Corner*.

Thanks to Mary Tiegreen, who gave me this opportunity to contribute to the lengthening list of books she has conceived, illustrated, and shepherded into print.

Thanks also to Jennifer Levesque, Leslie Stoker, and Michael Jacobs for loving the Masters as much as we do.

And thanks to my wife Beth, who contributed ideas for this book and who contributes greatly to my beautiful life. And to our kids and grandkids.

And finally, thanks to Bobby Jones for creating the Masters, and to the players who have never failed to thrill us.

ARNOLD PALMER'S EAGLE PUTT ROLLS CLOSE TO THE 13TH CUP BUT MISSES BY INCHES IN THE FINAL ROUND OF THE 1964 MASTERS TOURNAMENT. PALMER WON AN UNPRECEDENTED FOURTH MASTERS TITLE.

"If ever I needed an eight foot putt,
and everything I owned depended
on it, I would want
Arnold Palmer to putt for me."

Bobby Jones

Photo Credits

Pages 1, 2-3, 4-5, 8-9, 9, 11, 15, 16, 17, 19, 20-21, 22-23, 24-25, 25, 27, 30, 31, 40-41, 42, 42-43, 44, 44-45, 46-47, 47, 54-55, 56-57, 58-59, 60-61, 66-67, 68-69, 71, 77, 78, 79, 80-81, 82, 83, 84-85, 86-87, 88-89, 90, 90-91, 92, 93, 96-97, 100-101, 101, 103, 104-105, 105, 106, 106-107, 108, 109, 110, 116, 116-117, 118-119, 120, 121, 122-123, 124-125, and 126-127 courtesy of AP Wide World Photos.

Pages 6-7, 12-13, 26, 28-29, 32-33, 34-35, 36-37, 38-39, 48-49, 50-51, 64-65, 72-73, 74-75, 94-95, 112-113, and 114 courtesy of Historic Golf Photos, The Ron Watts Collection.

Pages 7 and 115 courtesy of Ron Green, Sr.

Pages 32, 50, and 128 courtesy of The Tiegreen Archives.

Pages 52-53 (photo by Jeff Janowski); 62-63 and 98-99 (photos by Rob Carr) courtesy of The Augusta Chronicle.

TIGER WOODS AND MARK O'MEARA WALK UP THE 7TH FAIRWAY DURING PRACTICE FOR THE 2007 MASTERS.

 A Tiegreen Book

Published in 2008 by Stewart, Tabori & Chang
An imprint of Harry N. Abrams, Inc.

Library of Congress Cataloging-in-Publication Data:

Green, Ron, 1929-
    The Masters : 101 reasons to love golf's greatest tournament / by Ron Green, Sr.
        p. cm.
    ISBN 978-1-58479-694-7
    1. Masters Golf Tournament—Miscellanea.   I. Title. II. Title: 101 reasons to love golf's greatest tournament.

GV970.3.M37G74 2008
796.352'66—dc22

                          2007032568

EDITOR: Jennifer Levesque
DESIGNER: Mary Tiegreen
PRODUCTION MANAGER: Jacquie Poirier

The text of this book was composed in Berkeley,
Medici Script, ITC Cheltenham and Centarra Nova.

Printed and bound in China
10 9 8 7 6 5 4 3 2

HNA ▌▌▌▌▌
harry n. abrams, inc.
a subsidiary of La Martinière Groupe
115 West 18th Street
New York, NY 10011
www.hnabooks.com